SERIES EDITOR: DONALD S

OSPREY MODELLING M

G000038863

North American P-51 Mustang

RODRIGO HERNÁNDEZ CABOS AND GEOFF COUGHLIN

OSPREY
MODELLING

First published in Great Britain in 2002 by Osprey Publishing, Elms Court,
Chapel Way, Botley, Oxford OX2 9LP United Kingdom
Email: info@ospreypublishing.com

ISBN 1 84176 267 9

Editor: Donald Sommerville
Design: Compendium Publishing Ltd

Originated by Accion Press
Printed in China through World Print Ltd

02 03 04 05 06 10 9 8 7 6 5 4 3 2 1

**For a Catalogue of all books published by Osprey Military and Aviation
please write to:**
The Marketing Manager, Osprey Direct UK, P.O. Box 140,
Wellingborough, Northants NN8 2FA United Kingdom
Email: info@ospreydirect.co.uk

The Marketing Manager, Osprey Direct USA c/o MBI Publishing, P.O. Box 1,
729 Prospect Ave, Osceola WI 54020, USA
Email: info@ospreydirectusa.com

www.ospreypublishing.com

Acknowledgements

The Introduction and Chapters 3 to 7 were written by Geoff
Coughlin.

Chapter 1 is by Juan M. Villalba Dominguez, Julio C. Cabos
and Antonio Morant Bohórquez. Chapter 2 is by Fernando
Garcia Buergo, Juan M. Villalba Dominguez, Julio C. Cabos
and Sergio Usera Mugica.

Linework by Carlos de Diego Vaquerizo.

Colour profiles by Julio C. Cabos, Eduardo Cea Ovejero
and Guillermo Coll Llopis.

Photographs by Carlos Salvador Gómez, Rodrigo
Hernández Cabos.

CONTENTS

INTRODUCTION

BRIEF HISTORY OF THE MUSTANG

The USAAF very nearly didn't get the P-51 Mustang at all, had it not been for the Royal Air Force requirement for an alternative to the P-40. The aircraft was subsequently hugely improved by the addition of a Rolls-Royce Merlin engine, again stipulated by the RAF. Finally, in this form it became highly effective as a long-range escort fighter, capable of seeing Allied bombers all the way to Germany.

The RAF initially took delivery of the Mustang I powered by the Allison engine. This aircraft was found to be quicker than the contemporary Spitfire Mark V, although it was never really regarded as an interceptor fighter – the Spitfire and Messerschmitt Bf 109 were both more manoeuvrable at higher altitudes for example. The Mustang's primary role was as a low-level tactical fighter and the type was first stationed at RAF Burtonwood in October 1941.

The remarkable similarity in size between the Allison and Merlin engine meant that only minor redesign of the forward fuselage was needed to test if the different engine would bring worthwhile improvements. The first Merlin-powered Mustang was flown on 13 October 1942 and the transformation was astonishing. Soon the P-51B entered service with the USAAF's Eighth Air Force, based in England. With drop tanks, the fighters could escort the bombers deep into Germany. The first victory came when Lt Charles F. Gumm of the 355th Fighter Squadron shot down a Messerschmitt Bf 110 over Bremen.

BELOW **RAF Mustang Mk I (P-51A), the version powered by the Allison engine, seen in action from a UK base in July 1942.**

A lack of visibility from the early Mustang resulted in the RAF's experimental facility at Boscombe Down fitting what became known as the 'Malcolm Hood' – a much improved blown canopy. This canopy was fitted to all Mustang IIIs flying with the RAF and many of those P-51Cs operational with the USAAF. Long range continued to be a major advantage for what was becoming a real thoroughbred fighter and round trips of 1,200 miles were common. Of the 2,828 P-51B/C fighters received by the USAAF, 71 P-51Bs and 20 P-51Cs were modified for the tactical reconnaissance role and designated F-6C.

Even more worrying for the Luftwaffe, was the fact that its Focke-Wulf and Messerschmitt aircraft had an equal with the arrival of the P-51D. This version of the Mustang was the most famous of the type, with many to be found still flying today throughout the world – a real testimony to the strength and design of the aircraft.

The P-51D had a much higher wing loading, carrying additional fuel and bombs. The Mustang began to be used in the offensive ground attack role, often after escorting the Allied bomber streams to their targets deep inside enemy territory. An incredible 42 US fighter groups were eventually equipped with the P-51D, some 1,500 aircraft in total. A total of 7,956 P-51Ds was built and these differed from the P-51Bs and Cs by introducing as standard a bubble canopy to provide the pilot with excellent all-round vision. They also featured a modified rear fuselage and an armament of six 0.5-inch machine guns. Those converted to the reconnaissance role became F-6Ds.

The Mustang mainly saw service in Europe, with few squadrons of the type operating in the Pacific Theatre. The huge Boeing B-29 Superfortress bombers attacking Japan did, however, need long-range protection and two Fighter Groups, the 15th and 21st were despatched to Iwo Jima specifically for that purpose early in 1945.

The P-51 saw service in many foreign Air Arms such as those of New Zealand, Canada, France, Sweden, China and various South American countries – many remaining in service long after the end of WWII.

In the immediate post-war years P-51s remained in US service also, particularly with Strategic Air Command, until 1949. Others served with Air National Guard and US Air Reserve units and were amongst the first

US fighters to see service in the Korean War. In addition, the Mustang was licence-produced in Australia but fitted with the Rolls-Royce Merlin engine rather than the American built Packard Merlin version. A grand total of 14,819 Mustangs was built.

BRIEF HISTORY OF P-51 MODELLING

Those of you who have been around the modelling scene for any number of years, will obviously be aware by now that there are some aircraft that have gained 'cult' status and the North American P-51 Mustang is right up there with the rest. We all have our favourites, but the Focke-Wulf 190, Messerschmitt Bf 109 and Spitfire are likely to be there, too.

Perhaps it is no surprise then that the model kit manufacturers over the years have looked to cultivate our interest by producing large quantities of these popular WWII fighter types. You really could write a detailed book on the development of the Mustang in model form, such is the range of scale models that has been available through the years. It is not our intention to do this here, though, merely to trace the history of the type in model form and get a taste for what is currently available.

Elsewhere in this publication (pages 59–61) you will find a detailed round up of all the kits and a selection of model accessories that are available at the time of writing in 2001.

We thought that it would be interesting to notice some of the landmark events that have occurred – releases that stand out over the years. Airfix set the scene back in the 1950s and later in the 60s and 70s by creating a range of models primarily in 1/72 scale. Way ahead of its time, the release of the company's huge North American P-51D Mustang in 1/24 scale and, before that, the Spitfire took the modelling world by storm. People often refer back to these early days as a time when the hobby was at its strongest. Arguably it was – certainly many younger modellers were involved in a hobby that appeals to all ages and abilities. The Mustang 'Super Kit' in 1/24 scale was important for many reasons, but it clearly set a standard, being generally accurate and crammed with detail – all possible because of the large scale.

It is rare to find an original 1/24 scale Mustang these days in second hand form at model shows and model shops around the world but they are still well worth looking out for. Having said this, Airfix have re-released the Mustang and, bar some sink marks here and there on the parts, the kits still holds its own today. One of the difficulties modellers have always faced is where on earth you can safely store a completed 1/24th scale Mustang? Perhaps that is why you do not often see many assembled large-scale models on the model club tables and displays at model shows around the world.

At the start of the 21st century, however, it is clear that there is renewed interest from many modellers in the larger scales – particularly 1/32. Hasegawa currently offers a very good 1/32 scale P-51D and it is good to see that Paragon has supplied several resin accessories in this larger scale.

As we said earlier, just about all of the major model manufacturers include one or more P-51 Mustangs in their range – Hasegawa, Italeri, Airfix to name a few. Another recent landmark development has been the release of the P-51 in a number of variants by Tamiya. If you are looking for a beautifully manufactured Mustang kit, then this range is hard to beat. Significantly they are accurate and come in the ever-popular 1/48 scale.

Quarter scale, as it is often referred to, is becoming very popular, particularly for WWII fighters. The reasons for this are often to do with the modeller wanting a decent sized model, but one that is small enough when completed to be stored easily without getting damaged. The smaller 1/72 scale has not been forgotten by Tamiya either as the company has now scaled down its excellent 1/48 scale model. Finely recessed panel lines and accurate shape are hallmarks of this manufacturer's recent productions.

BELOW **Hasegawa produce this very loud scheme for their good model in 1/32 scale. The box art is stunning.**

MODELLING EARLY MUSTANGS

Modellers really are spoilt for choice now with several models to choose from covering early North American Mustangs like the P-51, P-51A and B/C. Two examples are featured in this chapter. Late models of the type like the P-51D are in even more plentiful supply, and these are featured later in this book.

ABOVE **The narrow cowl and side-opening canopy are hallmarks of the early Allison-engined Mustangs, such as the P-51 seen here.**

P-51 MUSTANG

We begin with the first version of the P-51, equipped with the Allison engine and have chosen the 1/48 Accurate Miniatures kit reference 3400 to illustrate this article.

Although the detail is good in this model it has not reached 'state of the art' status as claimed in the

RIGHT **The sides of the cockpit had to be almost entirely rebuilt, because the kit parts have little relief and are not very realistic.**

FAR RIGHT **The seat was modified considerably, and all the missing detail was added.**

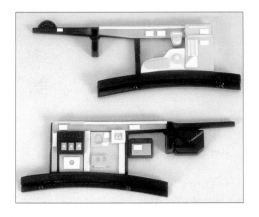

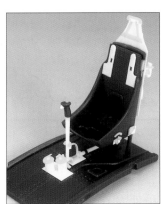

instructions. The injected plastic parts are reminiscent of the old Monogram kits in that they are hard to handle and have a tendency to shatter. There are extensive assembly instructions which are intended to be of great help to less expert model makers in understanding the sketches referring to the various stages of assembly.

LEFT **The rear of the seat was given new armour plating and the electrical components for the radio were also added.**

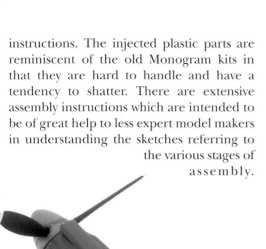

LEFT **The side-opening canopy is shown to good effect here – note, too, the yellow bands on the wings.**

Unfortunately the quality of these is poor and they are confusing. The later releases by this manufacturer are better, with more use of diagrams.

Assembly

We started by adding detail to the interior of the cockpit, since the parts the kit provides are too flat and correspond more to the P-51B Mustang than the earlier version we have chosen to make here.

We used acetate, plasticard and copper wire to complete the various areas, as shown in the accompanying photographs. As a reference source

9

RIGHT **We used acetate, plastic and etched metal parts to build the new control panel.**

we recommend *Fighting Colors* from Squadron Signal which can shed light on numerous queries.

It was necessary to add various details to the floor and we had to remodel the pilot's seat practically from scratch since

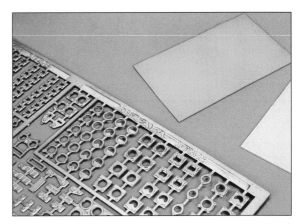

BOTH RIGHT **The photo-etched sheet can be used as a supplement. We built the frame and support panel from plastic, and acetate was ideal for reproducing the dials.**

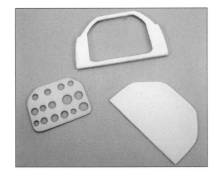
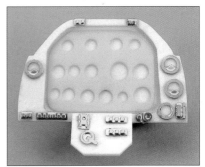

RIGHT **The pedals were made from acetate and plastic rods by Evergreen.**

FAR RIGHT **Finished floor, seat and panel before final assembly.**

BELOW **The early style USAAF markings are evident here, plus the high visibility 'Stars and Stripes' on the fin – removed on later Mustang variants.**

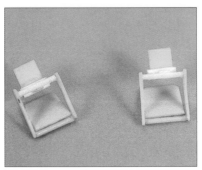

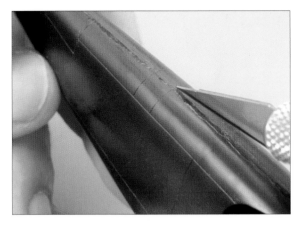

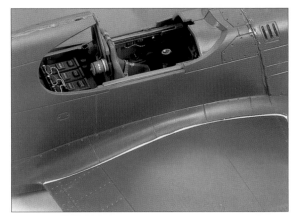

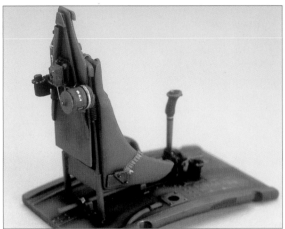

TOP ROW, LEFT **The fuselage was glued with cyano-acrylate, applied with a knife point.**

TOP ROW, RIGHT **Once the fuselage was assembled we checked that the cockpit interior was complete.**

ABOVE, LEFT **Electrical cabling was also added at the rear of the seat.**

ABOVE, RIGHT **The cockpit was completed by installing batteries and radio equipment.**

BOTTOM ROW, LEFT **View of the propeller blades before filing down: the shape and proportions are incorrect.**

BOTTOM ROW, RIGHT **To obtain the correct shape for the propeller blades we used various types of file.**

the armour plating at the back is too high. A new headrest and all the electrical installations to the rear were added once the original moulding had been filed down.

The front control panel was also totally rebuilt, because the Accurate part is transparent and would need to be completed using a decal for the back section. This system is impractical and, moreover, the panel has been poorly put together and the distribution of the dials is incorrect. To build a new control panel from scratch, we therefore used a 2mm piece of plastic, 0.2mm piece of acetate and a selection of photo-etched parts. Suitable sets are produced by manufacturers like True Details, Eduard and Aires.

TOP **Note the shape of the spinner and re-formed propeller blades.**

ABOVE **The exhaust weathering is particularly evident on this machine.**

OPPOSITE, INSET **The panels on the fuselage and wings have been gently sanded to give a weathered effect.**

OPPOSITE, MAIN PICTURE **The characteristic purposeful 'sit' of the P-51 is very well captured here – note the light grey undersides.**

We used 2mm Plasticard for the panel framework and background, with photo-etched instruments and dials. We painted the cockpit interior in US interior green FS 24151 with the front panel in matt black and detail in red, yellow and green for an aging effect. We used very dilute airbrushed black acrylic to shade the panels, and then dry-brushed with Humbrol grey enamel to create highlights, using a slightly lighter shade than the base colour. Once the cockpit was finished we proceeded to assemble the fuselage, fixing it with cyano-acrylate applied with a modelling knife. The assembly is not too complicated on the whole, and the pieces generally fit together satisfactorily. You will only need to fill in gaps at the main join of the wings. The filing down process was straightforward but also very time consuming, because of the very poor quality of the plastic which we mentioned previously.

The propeller that the kit provides is defective because the blades are too thick and wide and the blade tips themselves are rather too rounded,

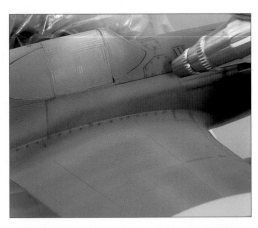

whereas those of our version were slimmer, longer and more pointed. You can use files and wet and dry paper to obtain the correct profile.

To build the guns we used a combination of hypodermic needles and PVC tubing for the barrels. The original guns have rings at their location which we decided to leave out, leaving smooth guns as in some Mustangs that saw action in North Africa.

RIGHT **You need to create a fine feathered demarcation between the grey and olive drab camouflage pattern.**

We added some new hydraulic lines to the undercarriage assemblies, which we made from copper wire and very fine cable sheath. To achieve the metallic finish we applied a base coat of Humbrol metallic grey No 56, and once this was

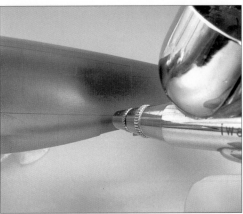

BELOW **The early olive drab camouflage provided reasonable cover when aircraft were dispersed on airfields.**

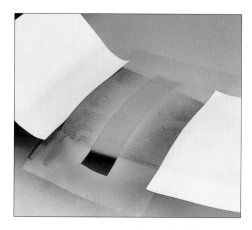

dry we highlighted it with a very dry brush and Tamiya matt aluminium XF-16.

Camouflage

We followed the colour scheme used by the Mustangs in North Africa which consisted of olive drab FS 34087 and neutral grey FS 36173, with bands in identification yellow FS 33538. To achieve this we used Gunze Sangyo olive drab H-304, Tamiya neutral grey XF-53 plus a little 105 white for the neutral grey, and Tamiya matt yellow XF-3 plus about 10% red for the identification yellow.

The edge where the olive drab meets the neutral grey was softened using a finely set airbrush.

The yellow bands were painted with the airbrush as were the personal names on the plane, in both cases using adhesive masking tape. The aging effect was achieved by highlighting panel outlines with black and sepia colours with an airbrush, and also by lightening certain panels and by weathering the exhaust areas using a lighter colour.

The decal application was straightforward. The only point to note was that a minimum of five hours' drying time was necessary before applying varnish, because the decals are rather on the hard side. The model was then finished off with a few light coats of Marabu satin varnish. AeroMaster or Revell varnishes would also work well.

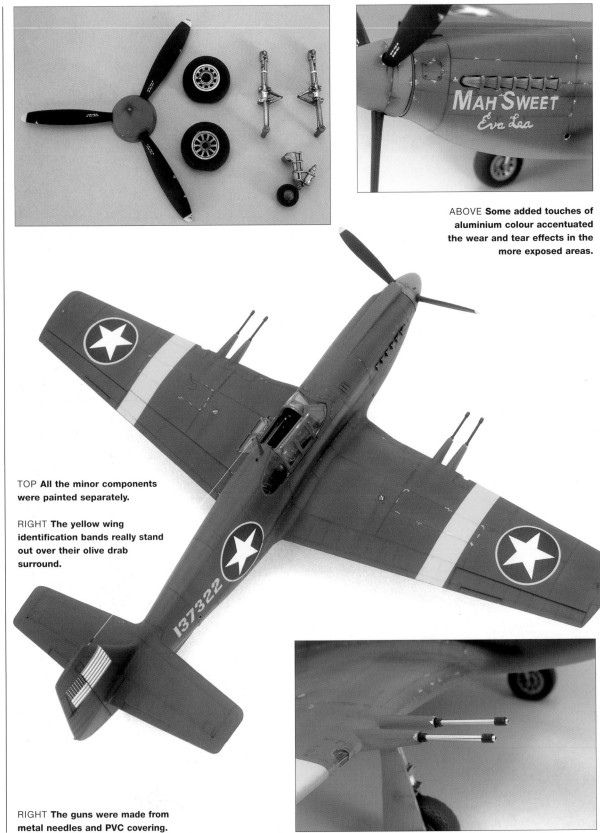

ABOVE **Some added touches of aluminium colour accentuated the wear and tear effects in the more exposed areas.**

TOP **All the minor components were painted separately.**

RIGHT **The yellow wing identification bands really stand out over their olive drab surround.**

RIGHT **The guns were made from metal needles and PVC covering.**

MAH SWEET
Eva Lea

137322

COLOUR CHART

	F.S.	Humbrol	G. Sangyo	Tamiya	Model Master	Molak
Matt black	37038	33	12	XF-1	1749	2M
Matt white	37875	34	11	XF-2	1768	1M
Aluminium	17178	11	8	XF-16	1781	26
Olive Drab	34087	155	304	XF-58	1711	34087
Neutral Grey	36270	176	306	XF-20	1725	36270
Zinc chromate	34227	120	312	XF-4	1734	34227
Yellow	33538	154	329	XF-3	1708	33538
Bright red	11136	19	3	X-7	2718	4
Bright green	14187	2	26	X-5		12
Bright orange	12197	18	14	X-6	2731	3
Gun metal		53	18	X-10	1423	25
Burnished metal			76		1415	

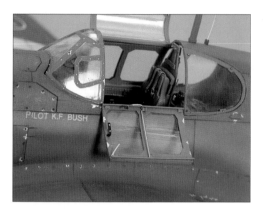

The cockpit canopy can be cut with a fine saw and the frame painted with the help of adhesive masking tape. We used interior green on the inside and olive drab on the outside. Finally we used small dots of white glue to attach the canopy correctly to the completed model.

LEFT **We decided to assemble the canopy in the open position.**

BELOW **Note the thin aerial wire – very fine fishing line works very well using cyano-acrylate glue to attach it.**

ABOVE **The distinctive yellow/ black checkertail of the 325th Fighter Squadron, Fifteenth Air Force.**

P-51B CHECKERTAILS

The early combat service of the first versions of the Mustang soon highlighted the short range of these aircraft and the poor performance of their Allison engines at higher altitudes. In 1942 it was proposed to install a Rolls-Royce Merlin engine to see if these shortcomings could be rectified. The result was spectacular. In the words of a test pilot, 'It was like driving a racing car.'

FAR RIGHT **The cockpit unit as fitted into the interior of the fuselage. The interior green ANA 611 colour can be appreciated, as well as the detail of various parts such as belts, first aid kit, (at pilot's shoulder level), etc.**

RIGHT **Another shot of the same area on the model. The wood has been imitated using an airbrush to give graded tones and has been finished off with fine lines in acrylic shades.**

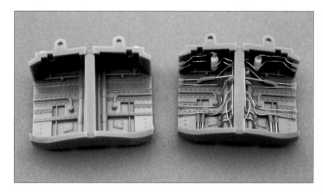

It was, without a doubt, the plane that the struggling US Eighth Air Force was looking for to escort its B-17s in their perilous sorties far over the heartland of the Reich. As well as having a much more satisfactory engine, the new fighter plane was equipped with an extra 322-litre fuel tank, just behind the pilot's seat. The increased fuel load allowed the plane to travel over Germany at will, but affected the centre of gravity of the aircraft to such an extent that it was seriously unstable. This problem was never satisfactorily solved, and required great concentration on the part of the pilot during the first part of a mission until the fuel in that particular tank had been used up and the plane returned to normal.

The first Merlin Mustangs were built as the P-51B by the North American Aviation plant at Inglewood, California (2,000 examples), and

ABOVE **The interior of the undercarriage wells was detailed using copper wire, telephone wire and plastic links. Compare the modified part with the original.**

LEFT **Here you can appreciate the colour nuances of the metal areas and the dirty condition of the engine exhausts (mixture of acrylic and very diluted brown) and the red spinner.**

as the P-51C at a second North American production line in Dallas, Texas (1,750 examples). Although the Dallas model was referred to as the 'C', it was identical to its Californian twin brother.

The Model

Of all the Mustang kits on the market (of which there are many) the Tamiya 1/48 representation of the Mustang B/C which we chose to use stands out in terms of quality. The Tamiya model has superb detail and clean plastic lines, fitting together accurately and easily. As a result assembling our Mustang model was a pleasure.

There are only a few areas in the model on which we can improve, notably the cockpit and the undercarriage section.

BELOW **Observe the tonal differences on the wing panels and the checkering on the tail in this view from above.**

Cockpit

This is possibly the poorest section the manufacturer has produced. The detail, although correct, is too spartan. The most obvious error is that the floor that has been represented as metal, whereas in fact all the Mustangs with a Merlin engine (versions B/C and D) had wooden flooring. To correct this, we had two options: to do it ourselves, or to use one of the many kits available on the market to improve the cockpit.

We chose the latter, opting for the Verlinden set. The resin parts are, on first impression, very good and this can be confirmed by comparing them with actual photographs of the plane's interior. The only way actually to fit them, however, was to get the minidrill out and take off all the original side sections of the model and then use up mountains of sandpaper and plenty of patience.

BELOW **View from underneath the plane. Note that the undersides of the tail are not decorated with the checker pattern.**

RIGHT We can see in detail the size and shape of the anti-glare panel painted in olive drab. This colour had a tendency to weather very rapidly, resulting in a variety of different shades. We accordingly augmented the original colour using various mixtures of yellow and white, gently applying the extra coats by airbrush.

BELOW RIGHT The nose section of the plane seen from the right. Note the absence of any personal insignia on this side of the plane.

BELOW The weapon access hatches are in a distinctive dark metal tone. To obtain this effect we masked off the area and mixed the SNJ with Tamiya XF-16 enamel.

BOTTOM RIGHT The three lights in the lower section of the wing were made by putting a transparent plastic tube near a flame. This gave it an oval shape. The inside of the glass cover also needed to be painted. We detailed the detachable part with plastic and small pieces of plasticard and all that remained was to paint the inside with the desired colour.

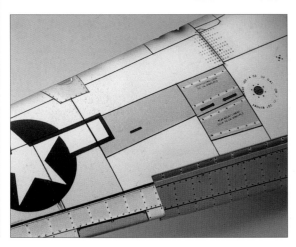

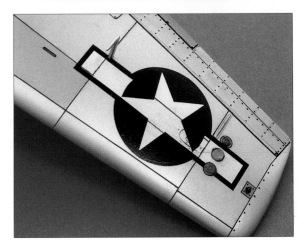

LEFT In this photo we can appreciate the detail on the undercarriage. We painted the insides of the doors in zinc chromate, although on some examples the inner faces were retained in natural metal.

Apart from the parts from the resin kit, we added a couple of etched metal items for the central section of the instrument panel and the pedals from an Eduard detail set.

Finally to complete this section of the model, we added some components that we had scratch-built: the radio battery and dynamo, (made from plastic strips) as well as the related cables (from 0.2mm copper wire).

Undercarriage

This part of the model was easier to work on than the previous section. Again we used details that we made ourselves. Using different widths of copper wire (0.2 and 0.3 mm), as well as plastic telephone wire, we concocted the whole network of wires, cables and tubes located within the undercarriage well. We also made two small canisters for this location, using two circular pieces of plastic. Finally we added the small tube for the brake fluid (copper wire of 0.2mm and plastic tubing) to the main wheel assemblies.

Once we managed to solve all these problems successfully, assembling the remainder of the model was straightforward.

Only the addition of small details then remained, such as replacing the machine-gun barrels with sections of hypodermic needle. Subsequently, after the main painting was complete, we added the lights, made from transparent plastic and Reheat parts, and finally put into place the locks of the canopy (scratch-built from small pieces of plastic).

Paint

In general the USAAF Mustangs had two colour systems during the war. One consisted of two tones: olive drab or medium green and neutral grey. Alternatively, especially on later examples, either no paint was applied to the aircraft, leaving the plane in natural metal finish, or aluminium was used.

RIGHT **The inside of the cockpit canopy also has to be painted. We detailed the opening part with plastic and small pieces of plasticard.**

BELOW **The lines of the P-51B are clean and the checkertail markings really stand out.**

COLOUR

	Federal Standard	Mix of Tamiya/SNJ	Area of model
Natural aluminium (shade A)		Aluminium SNJ	General finish
Natural aluminium (shade B)		SNJ + XF-16 (enamel)	Panels
Natural aluminium (shade C)		SNJ + X-11 (enamel)	Panels
Olive drab ANA 613	34087	XF-62 (acryclic)	Anti-glare panel
Interior green ANA 611	34151	XF-1 + XF-3 (acrylics)	Cockpit interior
Zinc chromate	23785	XF-4 (acrylic)	Undercarriage
Bright red ANA 619	31136	XF-7 (acrylic)	Propellers
Orange yellow ANA 614	33538	X-8 (enamel)	Tail & flaps

LEFT **The wheel wells were painted zinc chromate. The cables, tubes, etc. were painted using yellow, green and metallic shades.**

Achieving a realistic natural metal finish is a very challenging task. It is not easy to work in shades of silver. The paint tends to be unstable, volatile and very difficult to apply. Moreover the majority of ready made paints do not provide a credible or convincing finish.

Of all the options tested to date, we would recommend the aluminium enamel from SNJ Products. It is by far the best that today's market has to offer. The finish is very real, the pigment is imperceptible and most importantly it can take additional decoration. It is readily available from specialist suppliers like Hannants (see pages 63–4 for supplier details).

The first thing we need to do before applying the metallic paint is to polish the entire plastic surface of the model. Any marks such as scratches from sanding or remaining glue will be very unpleasantly evident when metallic paint is used. The plastic needs to be like a mirror. To achieve this we used superfine sandpaper and then rubbed the surface down with a polish such as Tamiya Compound or MER car polish. Any remnants of compound in the joins were then cleaned off with a soft bristle brush and plain water. Once this had been done we again cleaned the model thoroughly using alcohol, in order to eliminate remnants of grease and other impurities.

The paint should be applied in thin coats and does not require thinning. However, before filling the container in the airbrush, do shake the jar well to mix the paint components together properly. Remember that this paint is only for use with an airbrush. To achieve the slightly different metallic shades on the various panels, mix SNJ with Tamiya metallic enamels, specifically X-11 and XF-16, but in very small quantities.

Once the paint had been applied, we highlighted all the panelling lines and rivets with acrylic paints, (a mixture of black and brown) very diluted with water, and using the finest brush we had. Then the anti-glare panel just in front of the cockpit, was painted with olive drab, and the propeller tips with yellow.

Finally we varnished the model with the special varnish for metallic paint made by Model Master/Testors.

Decals and Insignia

Many American planes in World War II had extremely colourful markings. The famous nose art unit identification colours are a continuous source of inspiration to model makers. If we add to this the enormous range of decals available on the market, the choice for our particular Mustang becomes quite difficult.

We decided on one of the most eye-catching units of the Fifteenth Air Force: the 325th Fighter Squadron, better known as the Checkertails. Our specific Mustang was flown by Captain Robert M Barkey, of the 319th Fighter Squadron.

ABOVE **Detail of the tail section of the Mustang. We can appreciate in full the distinctive checkered tail of the 325th Fighter Squadron and the orientation of the black squares.**

We used the Super Scale decal set No. 480462. The quality of the decals is superb, and, if Micro Set and Sol liquids are used, the finish obtained will be perfect.

The Micro Set and Micro Sol liquids are formulated specially for positioning decals on any surface. They are very simple to use: first Set is applied to the surface which is to receive the decal, the decal is then positioned and Set is once more applied on top of this. Lastly, the decal is covered with Sol and left to dry. Occasionally the decal will wrinkle when the Sol is applied, but this is of no concern as the decal invariably reverts to its original condition once dry.

BELOW **Note the smooth nose contours of the Merlin-powered Mustang.**

MODELLING THE P-51D

This chapter features three model versions of the P-51D, all in 1/48 scale. The first two sections are based on the Hasegawa kit and the third on the rather older Monogram version. The two Hasegawa models are representations of the same aircraft with the same pilot's personal markings, but made by two different modellers and illustrating how different techniques and combinations of colours can achieve varying but effective final results. The third section on the older and less detailed Monogram kit illustrates detailing and finishing techniques that can be transferred to any representation of the Mustang fighter.

P-51D/HASEGAWA 1

Although its quality standards have been challenged by more recent releases from the likes of Tamiya, the Hasegawa P-51D Mustang (ref. J-15) is an excellent kit and good value, making it ideal for anyone who wants to add a P-51 to their collection. To help improve it we used the Eduard accessory set 48-15.

Cockpit

We began by assembling the cockpit and painting it in zinc chromate primer as for many American planes, mixing 50% Tamiya acrylic XF-4 and 50% XF-58. The instrument panel, switches, the wiring and engine controls were painted in black, as was the interior of the cockpit canopy frame, batteries and upper sections of the seat and the K-14 A gunsight. The latter has a coaming cover in front that can be painted in any shade of brown.

BELOW **The P-51D is probably the best-looking of the breed. What do you think?**

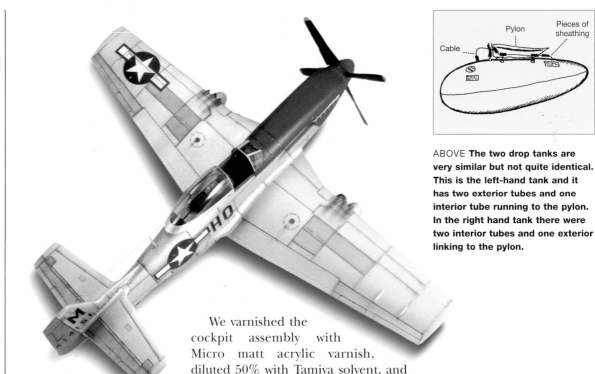

We varnished the cockpit assembly with Micro matt acrylic varnish, diluted 50% with Tamiya solvent, and left it to dry for a couple of days. We then put touches of black oil paint, very strongly diluted with essence of turpentine, into any nooks and crannies, removing the surplus a couple of minutes later (there is no need to hurry because it takes a long time to dry), using a flat brush slightly moistened in the turpentine.

The dry-brush work was done using a lightened shade of the base colour. We then added various details by brush with acrylics in the appropriate colours and highlighted some parts using Humbrol aluminium, which put the finishing touches to this whole area.

ABOVE **Be careful not to overdo the darker panels on the airframe or the panel lines.**

Assembly

As well as including some splendidly moulded and engraved parts, this is a model which could almost be assembled without glue, because the parts fit almost perfectly, so that putty is only necessary to hide joins. Even so, improvements can be made, starting with the brake lines on the main undercarriage assemblies. For this we needed monopolar cable of the type used as connectors in electric engines in toys. These lines tended to be located to the inner side of the leg and did not have a fixed location in a specific aircraft, particularly when it had been operational for prolonged periods.

BELOW **Note the accentuated panel lines.**

To make these we unsheathed a 3cm section of cable, (always longer than the leg) and straightened it. We then cut 1mm pieces of cable sheath and inserted them into the piece which we had straightened (3 or 4 per cable), without gluing them.We then glued one of these pieces of sheath and one of the cable ends, with cyano-acrylate. Once this had dried, we positioned it, placed the second bracket, glued the section of sheath, and repeated this procedure until we reached the lower end of the leg. On reaching the shock absorber and the end of the leg, we needed to leave a small piece of cable to be inserted into the hole that we had drilled into the wheel beforehand, as close as possible to the axle.

Whilst it was used as a ground attack plane in the Korean War, it was rare to see a P-51D equipped with bombs or rockets in World War II. Normally they are equipped with disposable fuel tanks, since their primary role in the conflict was that of escort fighter plane.

The fuel tanks used were either a 110 Imperial gallon capacity reinforced cardboard type or a 75 US gallon capacity aluminium one. We decided to model the latter type since it was more common. However, the kit comes with both versions, as well as 500-pound bombs, 5-inch rockets and triple 2.5-inch rocket launchers.

When putting the fuel tanks into place we noted that the tubes that connect them to the plane's internal fuel system do not run inside the pylon but are visible, so we assembled them as shown in the sketch, and along the same lines as the brake lines, except that the pieces of sheathing which we cut had to be 3 or 4 millimetres long in order to imitate pieces of pipe inserted into the tubing .

Painting

The undercarriage as well as the tail wheel and doors were painted using Tamiya acrylic XF-4 silver. The remainder of the plane was painted in XF-16 aluminium and varnished with Micro gloss acrylic varnish. In fact the P-51s finished in 'natural metal' only had this finish on the fuselage and tail, since the wing panels were primed, painted in aluminium and polished in order to retain their reflective quality. In any case, after a period in the air the shades became weathered and dulled.

We painted the rudders, flaps, ailerons and some of the fuselage side panels XF-4 supplemented by a mixture of XF-16 and X-10 gun-metal in varying amounts, since these assemblies used to be changed quite frequently in operational aircraft because of battle damage or other incidents.

We used the same mixture to paint the central inner panels of the main undercarriage doors. These can be assembled either open or retracted, depending whether the plane's engine has been idle for a long or for a short period of time. The main gear doors and flaps were on the same hydraulic system, so when one drooped, so did the other, a point of detail to note when modelling the Mustang.

TOP **Overhead view of the cockpit. A very delicate detail in this model is the antenna wire, which penetrates the transparent cockpit canopy.**

ABOVE **The panel lines and some details can be superimposed onto the base metallic colour. Various techniques were used: airbrush, oil washes, etc. Try not to overdo the effect.**

BELOW **The huge Hamilton Standard paddle blade propellers dominate the front end of the P-51D.**

ABOVE **The blue engine cowl and nose art are typical of US fighters of the period.**

If we examine photographs of the Mustang we can see that the doors can be in any position from 'fully raised' to 'fully lowered' and that when they are in intermediate positions, they are never quite symmetrical. The reason for this is that, when the undercarriage is opened, the doors come down so that the legs can be lowered; then the covers go up again, activated by their hydraulic systems (which work independently for each cover).

In this position (landing gear down and doors up) the plane can land and roll; however, when the engine stops the hydraulic pump whose pressure keeps the doors up also stops and the hydraulic pressure begins to bleed off, allowing the doors to lower so that after a while they are both completely drooped.

However, if we examine the fighter planes that operated in World War II we will see that, except for those built at the end of the war, hardly any of them have these inner doors (if you can see half of the wheel when the undercarriage is up the covers have not been fitted).

Having painted these doors we still needed to complete the panels around the engine exhausts, these tended to appear 'scorched' and we used a mixture of XF-16 and a small amount of XF-9 hull red to represent this. To finish off we painted the nose and the propeller spinner in XF-8 blue.

We next applied a coat of gloss varnish and positioned the decals (which are certainly very good) using Micro Set and Sol liquids. We then enhanced the panel lines with a soft lead pencil and the rudder, ailerons and flaps with very diluted black oil paint.

For the panelling we used very diluted acrylic XF-63 German grey (25% paint and 75% solvent), with 1kg pressure in the compressor and the nozzle of the airbrush practically closed, and the help of the familiar Post-it note to mask and protect the surrounding area.

After varnishing the entire model with Micro matt acrylic varnish, we glued the undercarriage and doors in place followed by the drop tanks and the cockpit canopy – having firstly drilled a hole in the canopy through which to pass the antenna wire.

Having reached this stage, and loaded the airbrush with a mixture of very diluted black and brown, we simulated the soot staining around the machine-gun barrels, as well as the stains left by gases emitted from the cartridge ejection chutes under the wings. With this same basic mixture made lighter or darker as needed we also simulated the discolouring made by the engine exhaust (which could vary from black to cream in colour depending on the consistency of the engine fuel).

The drips of oil and hydraulic liquid on the belly of the plane were simulated using very diluted black oil, using photographic reference, and we then finished off the model with some scrape marks using aluminium colour enamel on the engine cowling and particularly around the cockpit area.

P-51D/HASEGAWA 2

When building this P-51D, we opted to use the Hasegawa model, as explained above, complementing it with the surface detail kit from Verlinden Productions (ref. 1170) and using the AeroMaster decal sheet 48072. The basic Japanese model is excellent as a working base, particularly its fine and accurate panelling, well-conceived assembly and its cockpit canopy, which is of unbeatable quality.

ASSEMBLY

As usual, we started off by building the outline structure of the cockpit, using pieces of acetate and plastic. We then moved on to rebuild the side panels, floor, front panel and the support structures for the seat. Once this reconstruction was complete, we painted it all in interior green, using the excellent acrylic paint from AeroMaster. All the detail painting was completed using various shades of Vallejo acrylics but Citadel acrylic colours are also excellent. For the additional cabling we used 0.1mm copper wire.

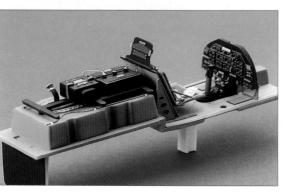

LEFT **The seat and main instrument panel were scratch built.**

LEFT **As well as adding the cabling for the batteries, we painted the cockpit floor to imitate the natural wood finish.**

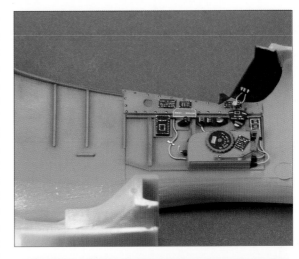

Once assembly of the cockpit was complete, we put the rest of the model together. The various parts all fitted together perfectly, making putty superfluous. One point of note was that we had to take particular care when we were assembling the various different component parts of the radiator.

Assembling the engine was quite a complicated task, and by far the best thing is to surround yourself with plans and all the documentation available with the model itself. First, we put the finely sculpted resin parts for the principal assembly in place; these are of a very

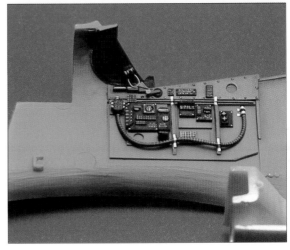

good fit, which allows any necessary adjustments to be made without problems. The engine is well put together and the moulding is very detailed. We then added the electrical cabling assembly and the cooling

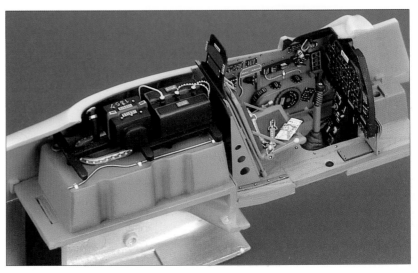

RIGHT **View of the cockpit, completely rebuilt. It is essential to check that it fits correctly prior to final assembly.**

FAR LEFT **The rear wheel well is shown after the various structures have been added.**

LEFT **Various circuits were added to the wheel wells.**

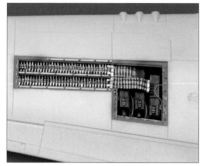

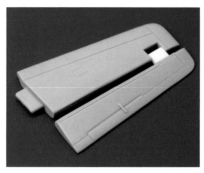

FAR LEFT **The kit parts are a perfect fit and simply require you to add the detailing.**

LEFT **The rear stabilisers were set up so as to give the model a natural look.**

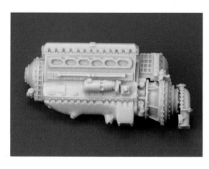

circuit, plus the innumerable couplings and brackets.

Finally, we attached all the latches and catches that make up the cowl. This is the most delicate phase as all the parts come photo-etched, making it tricky to give the section its correct form. To improve the detailing further we added a modification to the original engine, completely breaking down the panels that cover the carburettor induction pipe and rebuilding this part and all of its supports.

LEFT **Assembly of the engine is complicated but not too difficult, once you get a few shapes and proportions correct.**

LEFT **The covers of the gun compartments are photo-etched.**

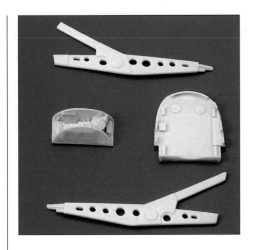

ABOVE **The engine bulkhead and engine brackets are resin parts.**

ABOVE RIGHT **The engine framing was painted in interior green and the support brackets in metallic paint.**

MAIN PICTURE **The open port wing machine-gun bay and access panel makes attention to this area an ideal subject for a model diorama.**

The resin detail set includes a good representation of the armament for the port wing. Once the access panels had been cut off, we put the resin nacelle in place. This is a superb fit and corresponds exactly to the interior structure of the wing. The 50-calibre machine-guns were painted separately and attached later.

Painting and Decals
We used SNJ enamel aluminium as our primer; this paint is easy to apply, does not need to be diluted and provides a magnificent shine and fineness

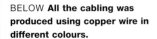

BELOW **All the cabling was produced using copper wire in different colours.**

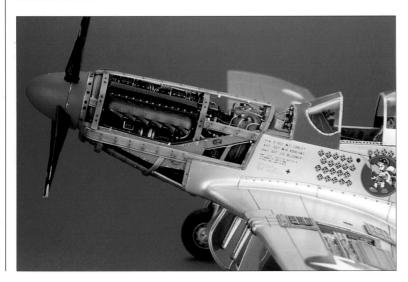

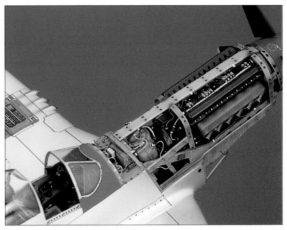

of grain. In addition it is very resistant to handling. We applied three fine coats at intervals of around fifteen minutes so as to cover the whole model uniformly. The differences in shades between the panels are obtained by mixing the SNJ paint with a tiny quantity of matt enamel aluminium from Tamiya.

We enhanced the model with a mixture of brown and black acrylic highly diluted with water and added to each recessed panel line and rivet using a 00 size brush. Finishing was carried out

ABOVE LEFT **The propeller spinner and anti-glare panel were painted medium blue.**

ABOVE **Painting the exhaust pipes in scorched brown weathering allowed us to create the impression that this machine was in operational use.**

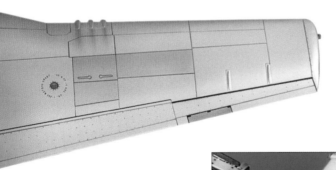

BELOW **The cockpit canopy and windscreen were given a shine using Tamiya polishing compound.**

ABOVE **This excellent close up shot shows off the detailed engine and undercarriage units.**

RIGHT **The wheel wells and the induction pipe are both painted in interior green.**

TOP **The transparent backing to all the decals was cut off, including for the tail numbers. This is often unnecessary as they are designed to blend into the paintwork.**

ABOVE **The carburettor induction pipe was totally rebuilt.**

LEFT **Brand names and 'stencils' were added to the tyres.**

RIGHT **The manufacturer's logos on the propeller blades are decals, whereas the 'stencils' were painted on with a brush.**

RIGHT **We darkened certain panels so as to differentiate between them.**

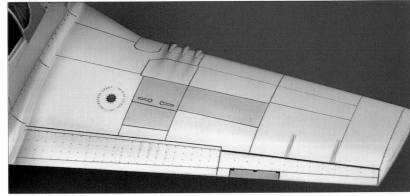

BELOW **SNJ produces a first class aluminium finish.**

using the sheet of AeroMaster decals mentioned above, which are ideally suited, although the decals have to be cut right to the edge. For the finishing touch, we applied a fine coat of the special Model Master varnish for metallic enamel paints.

As usual, we finished off the propeller, the undercarriage and the cockpit canopy separately, this last certainly fits like a dream. We also added the various caps on the radiators and the undercarriage at this final stage.

P-51D/MONOGRAM

The kit we used for this project is the Monogram 1/48 scale version. It is not a new model and indeed has been available for quite some time now, but the quality of the production is such – particularly in respect of the overall proportions – that it has not been too seriously affected by the passage of time. However, the interior, which seemed splendid when it was issued, has been superseded by the resin and etched metal detail in the Verlinden and the various other accessory sets currently available. Our chosen model is especially challenging because it involves extensive weathering which is difficult to reproduce in precise detail.

In order to assemble the cockpit to incorporate the Verlinden parts we needed to erase all the original moulded detail with a drill bit and wet and dry paper. We then assembled all the resin and metal parts, adding on some scratch-built items such as oxygen tubes made from rolled up copper wire. The interior paintwork was done in the classic bright green zinc chromate primer. The various controls and dials were then added using the illustrations on pages 41 and 42 as a guide. Enamel paint

BELOW **The Monogram kit is accurate and makes up into a good replica of the P-51D with a little extra effort.**

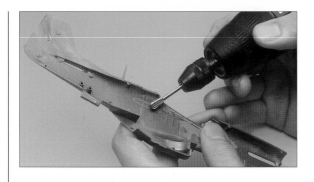

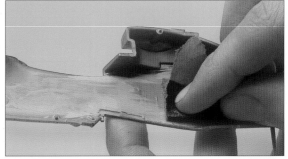

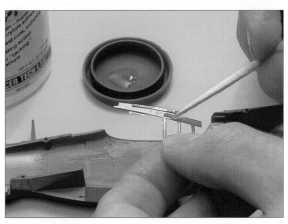

ABOVE **Unwanted detail on the cockpit interior was removed with a drill bit.**

ABOVE RIGHT **We then sanded off the remaining traces of the kit mouldings with wet and dry paper until the surface was smooth.**

RIGHT **The etched metal parts were cut out and positioned using cyano-acrylate.**

can be used to complete these, but most modellers will find that acrylics are more practical. More and more brands are coming onto the market, and it is usually simple to achieve the appropriate shades of colour by mixing.

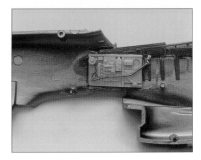

ABOVE, LEFT **The various resin components which form the cockpit sides were joined using cyano-acrylate.**

ABOVE, CENTRE **The glue should not be applied directly. Deposit a drop elsewhere and use this to obtain the amount you require.**

ABOVE, RIGHT **Some parts, such as the oxygen tube, were made using copper wire wound around another piece of wire.**

Exterior Paint

The fuselage of the later production Mustangs like this one was in a polished natural metal finish and the wings were painted in aluminium over the metal; the difference is hard to make out in a 1/48 scale model. The system we used to reproduce this is easy: it consisted of covering the plane with Tamiya X-11 chrome silver enamel, then giving it a sheen with X-22 clear varnish.

As reference we used the Squadron Signal book *P-51 Mustang in Colour*, by Larry Davis. This comprehensive monograph includes numerous profiles and interesting detail about the different versions. The aircraft we chose to model was flown by Lieutenant-Colonel Glen Eagleston, CO of the 353rd Fighter Squadron and top-scoring ace of the 354th Fighter Group, spring 1945. Since we did not have the appropriate decals to hand for this particular plane, we had to draw both the lettering and the distinctive personal markings ourselves.

The first task was to trace the code letters from the reference examples, transfer them onto adhesive tape, position them onto the

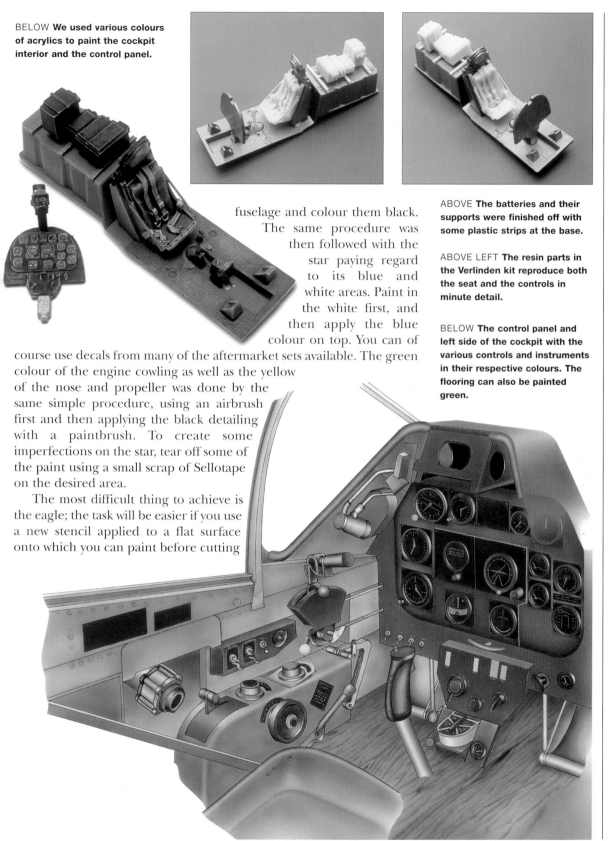

BELOW **We used various colours of acrylics to paint the cockpit interior and the control panel.**

ABOVE **The batteries and their supports were finished off with some plastic strips at the base.**

ABOVE LEFT **The resin parts in the Verlinden kit reproduce both the seat and the controls in minute detail.**

BELOW **The control panel and left side of the cockpit with the various controls and instruments in their respective colours. The flooring can also be painted green.**

fuselage and colour them black. The same procedure was then followed with the star paying regard to its blue and white areas. Paint in the white first, and then apply the blue colour on top. You can of course use decals from many of the aftermarket sets available. The green colour of the engine cowling as well as the yellow of the nose and propeller was done by the same simple procedure, using an airbrush first and then applying the black detailing with a paintbrush. To create some imperfections on the star, tear off some of the paint using a small scrap of Sellotape on the desired area.

The most difficult thing to achieve is the eagle; the task will be easier if you use a new stencil applied to a flat surface onto which you can paint before cutting

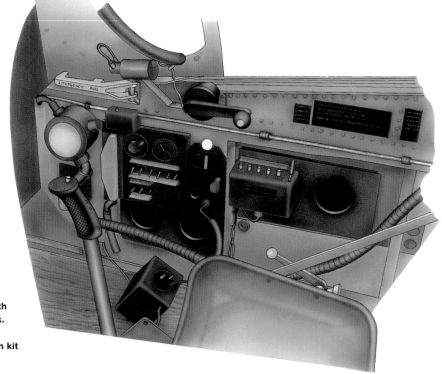

RIGHT **The right side of the cockpit interior with small touches of colour on some instruments.**

BELOW **The two side panels were painted in green zinc chromate primer. The instruments are in black, with delicate grey dry-brush work.**

BELOW RIGHT **The Verlinden kit also includes the parts for detailing the machine guns.**

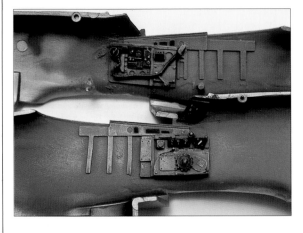

it out and then positioning it appropriately. The procedure we used was as follows: first of all trace the eagle's silhouette, then cut it out on the adhesive tape and paint it in dark brown, giving it a blue edge. Then proceed to paint

RIGHT **The open panels and the cockpit were protected when the model was painted with Tamiya X-11 chrome silver and varnished with clear X-22.**

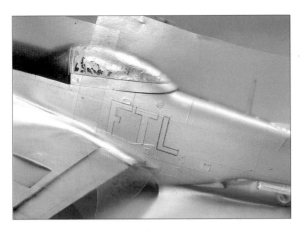

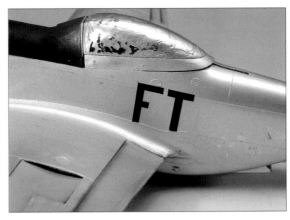

the white head, the feet, the beak and the eye in turn, outlining these very finely. The next step is to highlight the feathers in lighter brown, and finally give them definition with brown and white.

Panelling and Weathering

Among the interesting characteristics of the P-51 are the different shades of colour taken on by the various panels. These can be imitated by mixing chrome silver with a little gun metal which can be applied using masking tape to protect other areas. The edging of the panels can be represented by applying a grey wash, using the edge of a piece of paper as a mask tape to obtain clean lines. Alternatively you can use Post-it

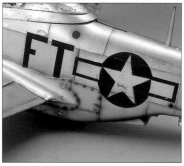

TOP, LEFT **The head, talons and beak were painted and finely outlined in black.**

TOP, CENTRE **The wings were given more volume using a lighter shade of brown.**

TOP, RIGHT & ABOVE, RIGHT **The shape of the feathers was brought out using a mixture of white and brown.**

ABOVE, CENTRE **The propeller was painted yellow and then black.**

ABOVE **Sepia tints were used for the stains on the panelling.**

BELOW **Access panels for the gun compartment were painted in a darker metallic colour.**

notes if your hand is not very steady, and these will stick to the appropriate area.

Stains and Dirt

All aeroplanes involved in combat soon began to accumulate oil and grease and dirt of various types. There were also other kinds of staining such as dust mixed with other elements, which could accumulate around the raised sections of moving parts, the rivets and at other parts of the airframe. The degree of severity of such staining was in direct proportion to the type and number of missions carried out. Generally planes designated for ground attack suffered more damage than pure fighter planes, although the latter naturally did not always escape damage either.

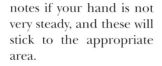

After studying numerous contemporary photographs in our reference books, we decided on the level and distribution of the dirt we were going to apply. This has to be applied very delicately, and only acrylics should be used, added with an airbrush or in washes. The best colour is sepia, applied in very controlled touches, using only a little paint and air,

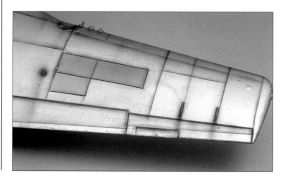

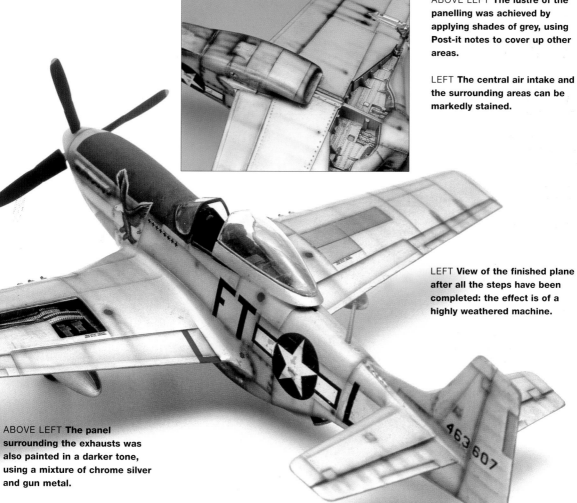

ABOVE LEFT **The lustre of the panelling was achieved by applying shades of grey, using Post-it notes to cover up other areas.**

LEFT **The central air intake and the surrounding areas can be markedly stained.**

LEFT **View of the finished plane after all the steps have been completed: the effect is of a highly weathered machine.**

ABOVE LEFT **The panel surrounding the exhausts was also painted in a darker tone, using a mixture of chrome silver and gun metal.**

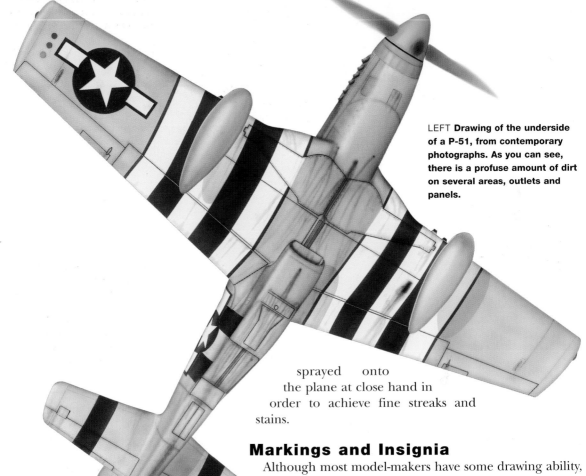

LEFT **Drawing of the underside of a P-51, from contemporary photographs. As you can see, there is a profuse amount of dirt on several areas, outlets and panels.**

sprayed onto the plane at close hand in order to achieve fine streaks and stains.

Markings and Insignia

Although most model-makers have some drawing ability, many will find it difficult to manage the proportions when drawing to scale. The simple solution is to use photocopies, which can be enlarged or reduced until they are appropriate for our model. To create insignia or markings all that is needed then is to transfer these to an adhesive stencil or a simple piece of adhesive paper such as a Post-it note, cutting out the outline with a craft knife. This system can be used not only for mascots but also for numbering and other insignia. Vinyl stencil material designed specifically for such a purpose can be found in specialist art

BELOW **Stains on flaps, ailerons, rivets and various panels.**

BELOW RIGHT **Undercarriage bay painted in olive green and olive gold, cables in grey.**

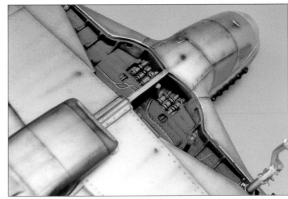

and craft shops. The task is then simpler since you do not have to draw onto the curved surface of the plane. It can be done on a flat surface, with acrylic or enamel colours, making sure that the coats of colour are sufficiently thick to give good cover, and then it will suffice to position the stencil in the desired area, in the normal way.

WALKROUND

1 Many P-51D craft have been preserved in an airworthy condition to the present day, although many of them bear colour schemes that are merely historical interpretations. Note how the flaps and undercarriage doors quickly droop when the engine is switched off.

2 This warbird is based on 'Short-Fuse Salee', a P-51B-1-NA piloted by Captain R.E. Turner, who scored 11 aerial victories and shot down two V-1 flying bombs.

3 The adjustable air outlet benea...

Aircraft shown in key is a P-51D

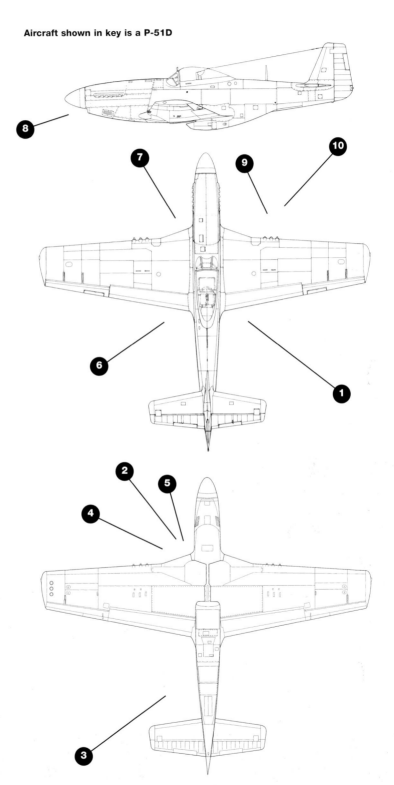

…e and the retractable tail landing gear.

5   Detail of the air manifold and radiator.

4   Interior of the wheel wells and undercarriage doors.

6   Note the shape of the panels in the wing roots.

7   Note the dramatic nose art and the shading differences on the engine panels. The exhaust outlets are protected with their individual protective covers.

8 Detail of the 'cuffless' type Hamilton Standard propeller fitted to the final Mustangs and commonly seen post-war.

9 Right-side undercarriage. We can also see the muzzles of the three 0.5in machine-guns.

10 Many P-51Ds can be seen flying in the USA at the Reno Air Racing Circuit – this highly-polished example may be a contender.

SCALE DRAWINGS

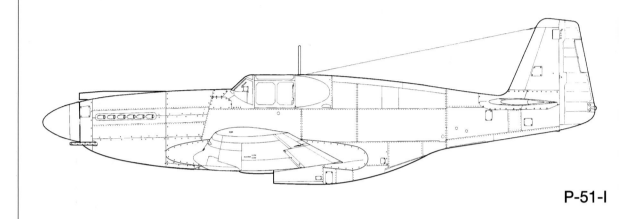

P-51-I

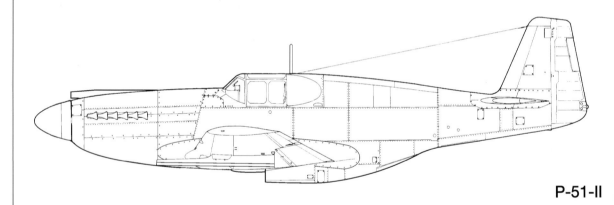

P-51-II

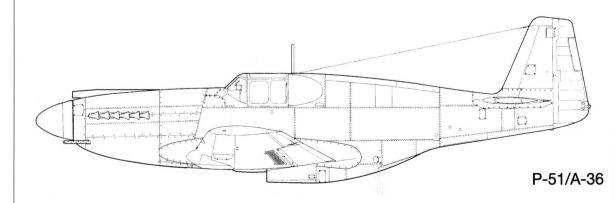

P-51/A-36

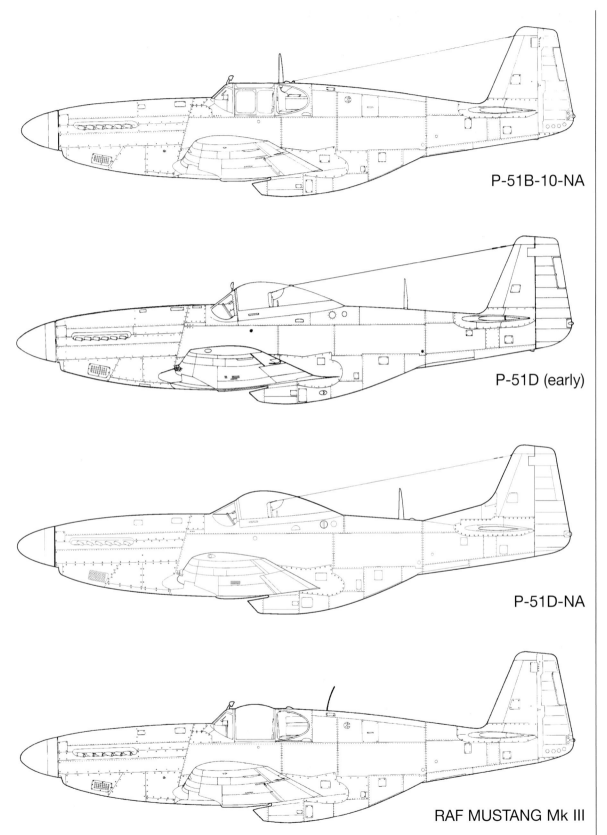

P-51B-10-NA

P-51D (early)

P-51D-NA

RAF MUSTANG Mk III

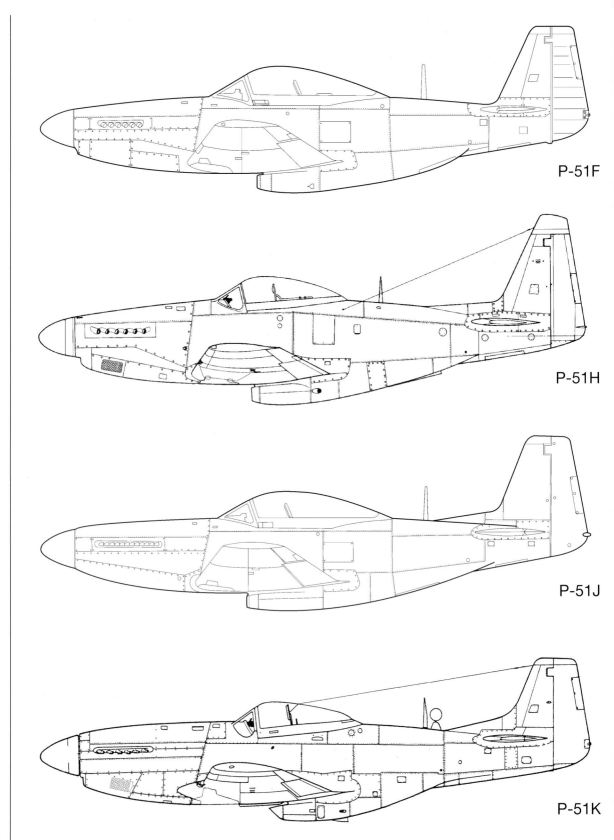

P-51F

P-51H

P-51J

P-51K

CAMOUFLAGE AND MARKINGS

If the RAF's aircraft were, by and large, relatively mundane and drab in appearance, then those of the USAAF were positively flamboyant. Particularly later in WWII, the natural metal/silver finishes of the P-51Ds and multi-coloured nose, spinner and tail surfaces singled out the American aircraft. Identification of friendly aircraft by Allied forces on the ground and in the air had always been important for obvious reasons, but towards the end of WWII in Europe, the Far East and the Mediterranean, air superiority had been secured, relaxing the requirement for effective camouflage. This resulted in more colourful markings being permitted and the development of these flourished.

However, USAAF aircraft were not always so colourful, especially early on in the war. The A-36 Apache, forerunner and first of the P-51 Mustang 'clan' initially received the appropriately named olive drab upper surfaces and light grey undersides. Yellow recognition bands were applied above and below the wings. The early Mustangs entering service with the RAF received standard camouflage of dark earth/dark green upper surfaces with light grey undersides. Later when the Mk III (P-51B) entered service, ocean grey replaced the dark earth and medium sea grey was added to the undersides. These RAF markings remained pretty much unaltered on P-51s from this point until the end of WWII.

The USAAF remained the major operator of P-51 Mustangs and, depending on their role, the majority retained a natural metal/silver finish on the fuselage and undersurfaces. However, most P-51Ds retained an olive drab anti-glare panel on top of the nose and engine cowl. Some aircraft also retained olive drab upper surfaces to the wings extending onto the wing root/fuselage join line as well as the upper surfaces of the tailplane. Many P-51s were committed to the close support/ground-attack role in Europe and those aircraft operating with the Eighth Air Force retained an olive drab finish on all upper surfaces. A red and

BELOW **P-51A-10-NA belonging to Colonel P.G. Cochran, commander of the 1st ACG, Tenth Air Force, India/Burma 1944.**

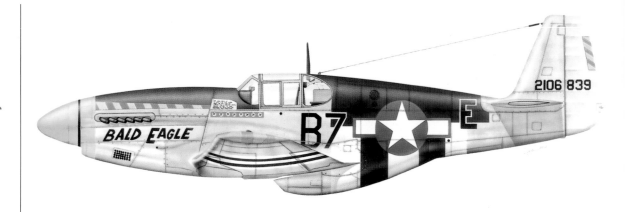

ABOVE **A P-51B of the 374th Fighter Squadron, 361st Fighter Group, Little Walden, Essex 1944.**

yellow chequered band on the tip of the nose broke this up, immediately aft of the spinner.

In April 1944 the P-51, along with other Allied aircraft involved in preparations for the D-Day invasion of France, had black and white stripes applied to the fuselage, upper and lower wing surfaces – three white and two black to each surface. The purpose of these was to ease identification by ground troops and friendly aircraft. With the success of the invasion, the need for high visibility markings on all surfaces lessened and as a result many aircraft had these markings removed from all upper surfaces. Even the underside wing stripes were mostly removed in August and September 1944, with those applied to the fuselage finally going by the end of the year.

Another interesting series of markings was applied to those P-51s operating with the Twelfth and Fifteenth Air Forces in the Mediterranean. Single, and later two, yellow 18-inch stripes were painted onto the wings.

A Group colouring system for the nose, including the spinner was introduced for all US aircraft in March 1944. The purpose of those markings was to ease identification of a particular Fighter Group's machines as they met up with their respective bomber formation whilst engaged in escort duties. These nose markings were very colourful and we have noted some specific examples below and illustrated others opposite. The black and white checks of the 78th FG in 1945 are well known to many. Others were: red and white nose checks plus a red/white striped spinner, 339th FG, April 1944; black/yellow nose checks with black/yellow stripes on the spinner, 353rd FG, December 1944; red/blue diamond pattern on the engine cowl plus striped spinner in similar colours, 356th FG, February 1945. These are just some of the many schemes added to the front fuselage of American P-51s.

The rear fuselage and tailplanes also received colourful, highly visible paint schemes. The 45th FS, 15th FG, had a broad green diagonal stripe outlined with black borders painted across the fin and rudder, plus the usual individual aircraft number in black beneath this. In addition, these stripes were replicated across the upper main wings and tailplane.

The 506th FG aircraft carried another example of high visibility identification markings. The 457th FS had the whole rear fuselage and tailplane/fin forward of the rudder painted red. Those P-51s of the 462nd FS had yellow in the same locations. A particularly striking

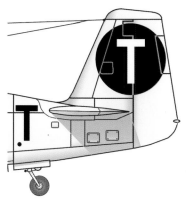

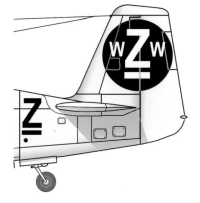

LEFT AND BELOW **A selection of markings and paint schemes from aircraft of the 20th Fighter Group, England November/December 1944.**

FAR LEFT **Tail of a 77th Fighter Squadron aircraft.**

LEFT **Tail of an aircraft from the Group's Operational training Unit.**

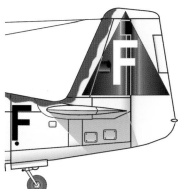

FAR LEFT **Tail of a 55th Fighter Squadron aircraft.**

LEFT **Tail of a 79th Fighter Squadron aircraft.**

BELOW **P-51D of 77th Fighter Squadron, squadron code LC, individual aircraft M, November 1944. Black and white spinner.**

BOTTOM **P-51D, 79th FS, December 1944. Black and white spinner with seven pairs of black and white stripes on the cowling.**

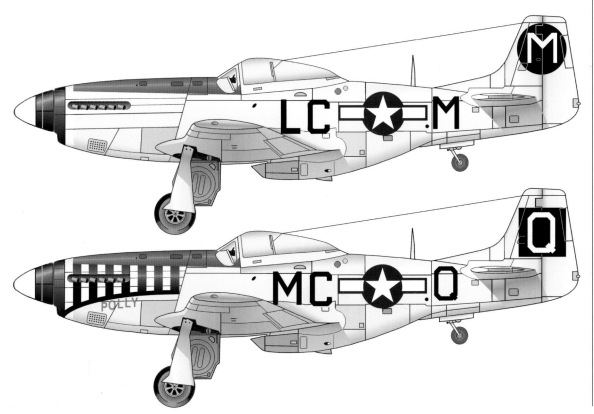

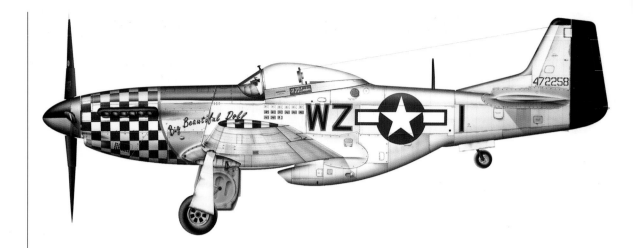

variation on this theme were the multiple narrow black diagonal stripes used by the 458th FS and again these markings were applied to the rear fuselage. A particular feature of the P-51 squadrons attached to the Eighth and Ninth Air Forces were the geometric squadron identification symbols painted onto the fin. Each individual aircraft letter was located within a black triangle, circle or square.

Some of the most colourful examples to highlight in this brief insight into P-51 Mustang colour schemes are the aircraft that flew with the 348th FG, Fifth Air Force. These P-51D aircraft carried three large broad black stripes above the main wings and two broad black bands around the fuselage aft of the cockpit. Furthermore, the fin featured a vertical blue stripe immediately forward of the rudder that in turn supported a series of horizontal red and white bars – very patriotic!

P-51s often carried the personal insignia of their regular pilot. Some examples are now very famous and the mainstream specialist decal manufacturers have produced many. A case in point is P-51D-10-NA s/n 44-14117, 369th FS, 359th FG, flown by Captain Joe Mejaski in late 1944 from East Wretham, England. His aircraft was aluminium overall, with the spinner and front tip of the nose in green. Recognition stripes were carried on upper and lower surfaces of the wings and horizontal stabiliser. Invasion stripes also appeared on the underside of the fuselage and a black and white skunk picture on the left side of the nose. Ahead of the skunk the word 'Stinky' was printed.

An example of an olive drab machine is P-51D-10-NA 'Tangerine', s/n 44-14507 C5*E of the 364th FS, 357th FG. Major Richard Peterson often flew this aircraft on ground attack missions. All upper surfaces were painted olive drab with light grey undersides. Major Peterson's aircraft were always marked 'Hurry Home Honey' and he was credited with 16.5 kills and 3.5 aircraft destroyed on the ground, making him the third highest scoring ace in the 357th FG.

Colour schemes were many and varied as can be seen from this short insight. Decal manufacturers will be kept busy long into the future, producing an ever-increasing range of markings for this famous fighter. Companies like AeroMaster, Cutting Edge and Superscale all have a wide range of P-51s in a huge variety of camouflage paint schemes and markings – you as the modeller simply have to choose.

MODEL ROUND-UP

The table and listings overleaf set out to provide you with an indication of what complete kits and aftermarket items are available for North American P-51 Mustang modellers. The P-51 Mustang is one of the most popular aircraft with scale modellers and so the main versions, the P-51B/C and D, are available in quantity from the manufacturers. In recent years there has also been a huge increase in the number of additional resin, brass, injection-moulded and etched metal accessories. A brief synopsis of the best ranges is given and, importantly, shows what is currently available in the UK at the time of writing in late 2001. It is always possible to miss something and if you are aware of available products not mentioned here, then tell other modellers who share your interest in the Mustang. Some manufacturers have 'promised' 'new' items for 2002, but many of these have been ignored because so often they don't actually appear.

This round-up would not be complete without reference to the magnificent range of 1/48 scale models produced by Accurate Miniatures. Although not so easy to obtain now, the A, B and C aircraft are amongst the very best on the market. It is particularly pleasing to be able to build the Accurate Miniatures' version of the A-36 Apache, forerunner to the P-51 Mustang.

KIT AVAILABILITY
This chapter describes the kits and other items that are available in the UK at the time of writing. Manufacturers and distributors, however, alter their ranges regularly, deleting some items, issuing new ones and making formerly discontinued products available once again.

Unfortunately this means that the kits used to produce the models described in the earlier chapters of this book may not be available by the time the book is published. These chapters should therefore be understood as describing general techniques, rather than giving instructions on building specific models.

Modellers who see kits they may need for future projects will often do best to buy them whenever they can afford to do so to ensure that they will have them available when they are needed.

ACCESSORY AND DETAILING SETS

We have listed below the main manufacturers of resin, etched metal and other conversion/accessory sets that are currently available, together with an indication of the kind of products they offer the P-51 Mustang modeller. An interesting fact is that several of the best resin and etched manufacturers, such as Eduard and Aires, are based in the Czech Republic. In many cases the standards achieved are truly outstanding. Some modellers seem to be put off by these high standards, perhaps fearing that they will not be able to do these accessories justice. This is a shame, because, with patience and practice, interesting and

BELOW **Who says box art doesn't sell scale models? These striking markings are offered on some realeases of the Hasegawa 1/32 scale kit.**

59

Complete kits by manufacturer

	P-51A Mk I/IA (RAF)	P-51B/C	P-51D	F-51	Other Variants
Academy ** G		7	7		
Accurate Miniatures ** A	4	4			4
Airfix ** G			2 4 7		7 (K)
Hasegawa ** A			3 4 7		
High Planes ** A			7	7	7 (H)
Historic Plastic Models ** G					7 (H)
Hobbycraft ** G			4		
Italeri ** A	7		7		
Minicraft ** G			M		
MPM ** G	7				
Revell/Monogram ** G		7			
Tamiya ** A		4	4 7		
Testors ** G			4		

Key
7=1/72 scale; 4=1/48; 3=1/32; 2=1/24; M=other scale

Skill Level and Accuracy Guide:
*** = For modellers experienced in using resin/etched metal   ** = Limited level of skill required
A = Accurate   G = Generally accurate

varied models can be produced that are different from the norm. By including these accessories the possibilities for diorama modellers are almost endless.

The following conventions are used: skill level and accuracy needed: *** = for modellers experienced in using resin/etched metal, ** = limited level of skill required; A = accurate, G = generally accurate

Aires *** A. This company specializes in high quality resin accessory sets, amongst the best on the market for detail. Their cockpit sets and engines are superb. A high degree of skill is required to fit the parts, but with patience the end result can be stunning. Aires sets haven't been readily available for very long but their impact on the model world has been huge.

Airwaves *** G. Airwaves etched sets are produced by E.D. Models in the UK. Most of the sets are formed from etched brass but resin accessories are now also available. The quality of the items produced has improved over the years and now a good range of parts and accessories for Mustang modellers is available.

Black Box *** A. Stormed onto the market in the last year or so with some excellent products – notably a resin cockpit tub for the P-51D.

Czech Master *** A. Details in resin and etched metal for the 1/72 scale modeller of the P-51A.

Eduard *** G. Eduard also produces kits, but is well known for the huge range of etched metal parts. The range is simply vast and you can spend many a long hour perusing lists of what is available. The P-51 Mustang modeller is positively spoiled for choice in all the major scales. Among the most useful additions are the etched instrument panels with acetate dials that fit behind the main panel. The effect is excellent and very realistic.

Falcon *** G. This company's replacement canopies are vac-formed clear replacements for the standard kit parts. They are generally very well moulded and clear but their greatest advantage over the kit parts is their scale thickness. They are much thinner than the polystyrene kit parts and, although tricky to remove from their backing sheet, add hugely to the finished model. This is particularly the case if you want to display your model with the canopy open.

Hi-Tech *** G. This French company has been established for many years and its resin detail sets will be known to many modellers. In some respects Hi-Tech set the standard for resin parts early on. They have some items useful to the Mustang modeller, particularly those who are building examples of the B model.

Paragon *** A. This excellent resin and etched brass manufacturer has plenty to offer the P-51 modeller – with flaps and cockpit replacements all available and in the larger 1/32 scale, too.

Reheat *** G. Reheat (along with Eduard) probably has the top name when it comes to etched instrument panels, placards and dials, and the like. The range is vast and it is easier to say go and look at the full listing. The sets invariably compliment those resin detail sets that you might use from other manufacturers and are well worth investigating if you are unfamiliar with them.

Squadron Signal *** G. What we've said above relating to Falcon canopies is equally relevant here. A good range overall with several types of Mustang hood available.

True Details *** G. This company offers a good range of resin and etched metal cockpit parts for the P-51 modeller. The hallmark, however, is the range of weighted tyres that is available. They seem to have established somewhat of a niche here with very few of the other manufacturers offering weighted tyres. Just occasionally, the 'flats' on these tyres look a little too flat so it is always worth checking this out with your references.

Verlinden Productions *** G. This long-established manufacturer provides some good sets for the P-51 modeller. The main contribution has to be the major sets to detail the Hasegawa quarter scale P-51B and D kits. The kits are greatly enhanced by the addition of these sets.

ABOVE **The Tamiya P-51D in 1/48 scale – a truly excellent model.**

BELOW **The 'checkertail' P-51D is featured elsewhere in this book. This is the box art from one of Hasegawa's releases in quarter scale.**

REFERENCES

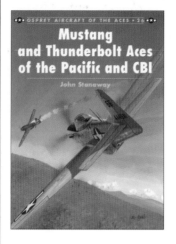

BIBLIOGRAPHY

Osprey's excellent **Aircraft of the Aces** series includes three useful titles: ***Mustang Aces of the Eighth Air Force***, ***Mustang Aces of the Ninth and Fifteenth Air Forces and the RAF*** and ***Mustang and Thunderbolt Aces of the Pacific and CBI***. These thoroughly researched volumes include good colour side profile views of different aircraft that can be used as the basis of modelling projects. By definition, the main aces' aircraft are well represented. From a modeller's perspective, they are great inspiration to go away and track down the specialist decal sheets relating to the aircraft of the particular ace you are interested in.

Aero Detail 13, North American P-51D Mustang, published by Dai Nippon Kaiga Co, Japan. This series is known to many and, although expensive, the publications are simply stunning references for modellers. Full colour, close-up photography and plans, line drawings as well as camouflage schemes make them irresistible.

Walk Around P-51D, *Fighting Colours* and *P-51 Mustang in Colour* published by Squadron Signal. The Squadron Signal publications are a must ofr modellers, mainly because of their clear presentation and breakdown of the features of the aircraft type represented. These examples have colour close-up photographs of surviving aircraft from museums around the world and in addition, feature good quality black and white pictures showing weathering and variations in camouflage.

Wings of Fame, Volume 1, published by Aerospace Publishing. This series of publications is current and known to modellers because of the detailed attention given to specific aircraft types. Volume 1 was obviously the first issued and as such the quality is exceptional. The main interest here for modellers is that this issue contains a detailed development history for the P-51. There are many invaluable colour wartime photographs, together with an excellent section on camouflage patterns with colour profiles of many different aircraft. In addition, it contains good reference material for the later P-51 variants such as the F-51D and H. Many overseas operators of the Mustang are included through text and colour photographs.

MUSEUMS

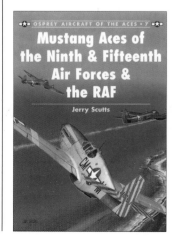

Surprisingly few original North American P-51 Mustangs remain on view in the UK. There are, of course numerous Mustangs at many locations in the United States. Many are in flying condition, with the type remaining extremely popular at air shows or in the unique Reno Air Races.

Those that survive in the UK are as follows:

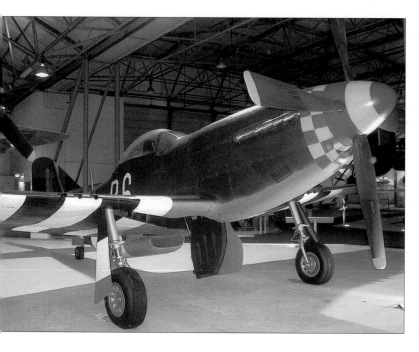

East Essex Aviation Museum, Clacton-on-Sea, Essex: P-51D Mustang 44-14574.

The Fighter Collection (based at the Imperial War Museum, Duxford, Cambridgeshire): North American P-51C/D Mustang 2106449.

Old Flying Machine Company (also based at Duxford): P-51D 463221 and Mustang Mk 22 (CAC) 472218.

The Imperial War Museum, London: P-51D 472258.

Royal Air Force Museum, London: P-51D 413573.

WEB SITES AND USEFUL ADDRESSES

Hyperscale (**www.hyperscale.com**) is excellent for build articles and technical information/reviews. An information request service is available, too, through other users of the site.

The **International Plastic Modellers Society** has a wide network of branches and special interest groups throughout the world. Membership of the British section of the society also brings access to The IPMS (UK) Modelling Weekend each year plus many regional shows organised by the various branches. Technical Advisory service plus member's Decal Bank are also features. For information contact the Membership Administrator: Sue Allen, 8 Oakwood Close, Stenson Fields, Derby DE24 3ET; www.users.globalnet.co.uk/~ipmsuk.

STOCKISTS

One of the best UK stockists, with just about everything for the modeller is **Hannants**, Harbour Road, Oulton Broad, Lowestoft, Suffolk, NR32 3LZ; tel: 01502 517444; fax: 01502 500521; www.hannants.co.uk. Also well worth noting are **Historex Agents**, the UK distributor of Verlinden products, Wellington House, 157 Snargate Street, Dover, Kent, CT17 9BZ; tel: 01304 206720; fax: 01304 204528;

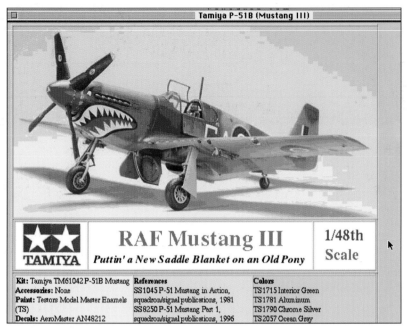

ABOVE The internet can be used to track down a wide range of product reviews, like this article from www.squadron.com, the website of a well known online stockist.

BELOW Websites help manufacturers and suppliers give full details of their products so that you can be sure what you are getting when you buy online. At the AeroMaster site, for example, you can view exactly what each decal set includes.

email: sales@historex agents.demon.co.uk. Another good stockist/mail order source is **The Aviation Hobby Shop**, 4 Horton Parade Horton Road, West Drayton Middlesex UB7 8EA; tel 01895 442123; fax: 01895 421412.

Hannants also stocks a wide range of accessories from a number of makers including the excellent **AeroMaster** decals (you can also contact the company direct at www.aeromaster. com); **Cutting Edge Modelworks/Meteor Productions** for resin, etched items, decals (also contactable at www.meteorprod.com) and **Eagle Editions Ltd** a specialist reference/decal supplier (also contactable at www.eagle-editions.com). **Airwaves** etched brass and resin items can be obtained from E.D. Models, 64 Stratford Road, Shirley Solihull, B90 3LP, England; tel: 0121 744 7488; fax: 0121 733 2591; email airwaves@ultramail.co.uk.

BOOKS AND MAGAZINES

Anyone who has seen *Tamiya Model Magazine International* will know about the generally high quality of production and interest in USAAF aviation projects. Contact ADH Publishing, 31 High Street, Hemel Hempstead, Herts., HP1 3AA; tel: 01442 236977; fax 01442 236988; e-mail ModMagInt@aol.com.

Military In Scale - Model Magazine is good for reviews and specialist articles. Contact: *Military In Scale* Traplet Publications Ltd Traplet House, Severn Drive Upton-on-Severn, Worcs. WR8 0JL; tel: 01684 594505 fax: 01684 594586; e-mail mis@ traplet.co.uk.

Midland Counties Publications is an excellent specialist book supplier: Unit 3, Maizefield, Hinckley, Leics. LE10 1YF; tel: 01455 233747 e-mail: midlandbooks@ compuserve.com.

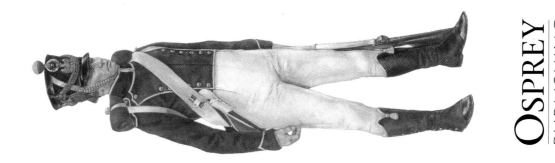

FIND OUT MORE ABOUT OSPREY

❏ Please send me the latest listing of Osprey's publications

❏ I would like to subscribe to Osprey's e-mail newsletter

Title/rank

Name

Address

Postcode/zip   state/country

e-mail

I am interested in:

❏ Ancient world
❏ Medieval world
❏ 16th century
❏ 17th century
❏ 18th century
❏ Napoleonic
❏ 19th century

❏ American Civil War
❏ World War I
❏ World War II
❏ Modern warfare
❏ Military aviation
❏ Naval warfare

Please send to:

USA & Canada:
Osprey Direct USA, c/o MBI Publishing, P.O. Box 1,
729 Prospect Avenue, Osceola, WI 54020

UK, Europe and rest of world:
Osprey Direct UK, P.O. Box 140, Wellingborough,
Northants, NN8 2FA, United Kingdom

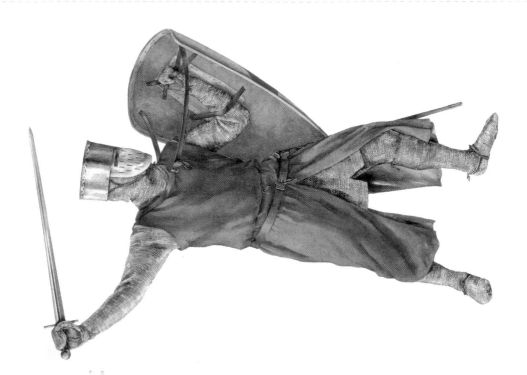

OSPREY
PUBLISHING

www.ospreypublishing.com

call our telephone hotline
for a free information pack

USA & Canada: 1-800-826-6600
UK, Europe and rest of world call:
+44 (0) 1933 443 863

Young Guardsman
Figure taken from *Warrior 22:
Imperial Guardsman 1799–1815*
Published by Osprey
Illustrated by Richard Hook

Knight, c.1190
Figure taken from *Warrior 1: Norman Knight 950 – 1204 AD*
Published by Osprey
Illustrated by Christa Hook

POSTCARD